GRIEF

GRIEF

SUZI EVANS

DISCLAIMER:

The content in this book is designed to provide helpful information on the subjects discussed. This book is not meant to be used, nor should it be used, to diagnose or treat any mental health condition. For diagnosis or treatment of any mental health problem, consult your own physician. The publisher and author are not responsible for any specific mental health needs that may require medical supervision and are not liable for any damages or negative consequences from any treatment, action, application, or preparation to any person reading or following the information in this book. References are provided for informational purposes only and do not constitute endorsement of any websites or other sources. Readers should be aware that the websites listed in this book may change and many people's names and identifying characteristics may have been changed for privacy.

Copyright © 2023 by Suzanne Evans

ISBN: 978-0-6459480-2-8

Book Writing Coach: Juliet Lever
Editor: Emma Offler
No reproduction without permission. All rights reserved.
www.kaizenb.com

The author and publishers have made all reasonable efforts to contact copyright-holders for permission and apologise for any omissions or errors in the form of credits given. Any corrections required should be submitted in writing to suzi@kaizenb.com

In Memory

To my beautiful Muzz

I thank you for the 29 years that I was blessed to have you in my life. You have given me so much to live for both before and after your passing.

See you in my dreams.

Love you, Mummy xx

> 'Maya Angelou, Nikki Giovani,
> turn one page and there's my mummy!'
> –*Hey Mama, by Kanye West*

Dedication

I dedicate this book to my husband Mick, for believing in me even when I didn't believe in myself, and for your unconditional love and selflessness.

You put my faith back in humanity.

> 'Every time I look into your loving eyes,
> I see a love that money just can't buy'
> - Roy Orbison

Table of Contents

Introduction 1

Chapter 1 - Shock 5

Chapter 2 - Reality 13

Chapter 3 - Trying to Make Sense of it All 21

Chapter 4 - Muzza's Happy Hour 27

Chapter 5 - Forgiving Myself and Others 33

Chapter 6 - Moving Forward 43

Chapter 7 - You Can't Pour From an Empty Cup .. 53

Chapter 8 - Living in the Now 59

Conclusion 69

References 81

About the Author 85

Thank You 87

Introduction

This is my story of grief.

In 2018, I lost my only child in sudden circumstances.

My son, Muzz took his own life two months before his 30th birthday. The grief I still experience to this day has changed me deeply.

Grief is a fact of life and yet it too often catches us off guard. I have written this book on grief to honour my son's legacy and to share the knowledge with you that I wish I had known along the way.

After I lost Muzz I found it difficult to find any information that resonated with me. I felt deeply lost and alone. Even though I had so much love and support around me, it was a loneliness that has been difficult to articulate. Along the way, in my search for some kind of sense and meaning, I started journaling. Writing my thoughts down helped me heal, so I kept going and finally just decided to collate these thoughts into a book in the hope that it may help someone else with navigating their grief.

After I lost Muzz, my journey to find my meaning and purpose in my life took a direction into healing, and along the way I learnt and developed an understanding that our emotions are all valid. Understanding how the brain, body and emotions are all linked allowed me to know how to manage my behaviour and reactions to my emotions more effectively through studying positive psychology and wellbeing.

This awareness, along with my studies, have helped me cope with my grief immensely and, through that, I developed a deep passion to help people learn how to be the best versions of themselves. So much so that I became a certified facilitator, trainer and coach in positive psychology and wellbeing and mental health first aid, and have also studied Neuro-Linguistic Programming.

Walking the path of grief is not easy. This is the book I truly needed when my son Muzz died. I wanted a book that helped me feel understood, a book that is easy to read on a plane, or keep by the bedside table and pick up over and over again when you feel alone. I have written this book in everyday language to try and make sense of grief and help you learn how to put one foot in front of the other each day. My hope is that it can also support you to understand someone who is going through grief.

The passing of Lisa Marie Presley in early 2023 hit me harder than I would ever have expected. Maybe it was because she had lost her son to suicide three years prior, and I felt some kind of unspoken bond between us. I thought to myself at one stage, 'God, if someone like Lisa Marie with all her resources couldn't save her son from taking his life, what hope did I have of saving my Muzz?'. In a piece she wrote for People magazine. published in August 2022, she opened up about losing her son. She shared, 'grief doesn't end, it is a lonely experience and you become part of a club'. I agree with her. Grief is a club none of us want to be a part of, but inevitably we all join.

Grief is a fact of life. We are all going to lose someone we love at some point in our lives. But how do we handle it? How do we cope? How do we realise we are not alone with our grief?

This has inspired me to share my book *GRIEF* in honour of my son's legacy, so I can help you feel less alone and more supported on your journey.

I hope it helps you.

Thank you for reading my story.

Suzi

'You will find life's pathway very rough in places, bumps and stony patches and jagged rocks sticking up, you will fall and get bruised but when you get to your feet again, just stand where you are for a few minutes and look about you and you will notice everything that grows, looks up to God. Before going on if you look again, you will notice if you lift your feet up more firmly you can step over those jagged rocks and put your feet down between them on level ground.'

My great great grandmother Harriet.

CHAPTER ONE

SHOCK

'Our children live or die with or without us. No matter what we do, no matter how we agonize or obsess, we cannot choose for our children whether they live or die. It is a devastating realization, but also liberating. I finally chose life for myself.'
- David Sheff, Beautiful Boy

Monday, 8 January 2018

It was a typical hot dry Mallee summer's day. My husband, Mick had done his usual check of the sheep and water in the morning and then called it a day early in the afternoon. Moments after we finished our dinner, we heard the dogs barking and realised a vehicle was approaching the farmhouse.

Grief

I went and looked out and saw a police car pulling into the driveway. I was confused, and said to Mick, 'it's the police, but it's after 7 o'clock?'

I thought they must have been coming to do a random farm gun check as we had heard news of these happening on other farms in the area at the time. I was in my nightie so I stayed in the house while Mick went out to speak to the policeman. They spoke for a while, and I began to get curious. I threw some clothes on and went out to see what was happening. The policeman was in the patrol car and Mick was standing back, looking not quite himself. He had one arm folded and was holding the other hand up to his face. I stood out under the pergola, just watching, to try to figure out what was happening. The policeman got out of the vehicle slowly. He didn't go to the shed to check the guns like I expected, but instead he started to walk towards me. I didn't understand what was happening.

'Suzi?' The policeman enquired.

I responded with, 'yes'.

'Your son is Murray James Chesser?'

'Yes.' I swallowed.

I started to get a bad feeling in the pit of my stomach. I felt like the policeman was talking around me like I wasn't there. I was lost in my thoughts, not knowing if what was happening was real or not.

The policeman even confirmed Muzz's date of birth with me, the 3rd of March 1988.

'Have you been contacted by someone else?' he asked.

'No.'

He told me there had been an incident and Murray had passed away that he allegedly had taken his own life.

In that moment, I froze. My feet felt like concrete, I didn't know what to say or do.

I swallowed and said, 'okay' as I tried to process.

Poor Mick had been told that Muzz had died but he wasn't allowed to tell me as the police had to — this was why he stayed outside for so long.

Grief

What a horrible experience for him.

The policeman said that they prefer to deliver this kind of tragic news in person, not over the phone and that is why the police station nearest to the incident, Jimboomba, had contacted the Waikerie police station to come and see me.

I really can't remember much of what happened next—all the things you hear and read are true, it was like an out of body experience or a movie playing in very slow motion. I don't know what I thought or felt. The policeman and Mick spoke about who Mick had to contact and what to do from there, then the policeman left and Mick and I went inside and sat at the kitchen table.

'I will never have grandchildren,' was the first thing I said.

I don't know why I said that, it just came out.

Mick was unbelievable—my absolute rock. He phoned my younger brother to tell him of the horrific news and asked him to let our parents know, my brother also had to let his own family know that Muzz had died. What a horrific experience for him to have to deliver that news.

Mick said, 'come on, and grabbed me by the hand. He took me up to where Muzz's dog, Milly was buried and we stood there for a while in silence. He said he didn't know what to do and that going to see Milly was all he could think of.

When we came back, there were messages on the answering machine from both my mum and dad and my older brother. I couldn't talk to anyone, I was in total shock.

For most of us, grief catches us by surprise. I personally hadn't experienced much grief in my early years – my only real recollection was at the age of around 12 with the loss of our family Labrador Cindy. I remember lying with my head on her back in the back of our ute, feeling so sad that we were going to say good bye. This disbelief and emptiness were my first encounter with the shock of grief.

I particularly resonate with the way Mary Frances O'Connor explains that no one can know what it is going to be like to walk through the world without the person they have lost. She has studied grief from the brain's perspective and in her book *The Grieving Brain* she describes grief as a heart wrenching, painful problem for the brain to solve. Her perspective is that grieving is a process of you trying to learn to live in the world with the absence of someone you love deeply who was ingrained into your life and your world.

This is why grief is so confusing to navigate. It's because the brain is literally trying to figure out where this person is now in our day-to-day life. The person lives on inside our memory and as such, the habits, the triggers and the associations we have with this person are still active in our brain and emotions.

The incredible resource, the Beyond Blue website www.beyondblue.org.au provides a lot of insight around understanding grief. They share the idea that, the more significant the loss, the more intense the grief is likely to be. Grief really does have no set pattern. Everyone experiences grief differently. Some of us may grieve for weeks and months, while others may describe their grief lasting for years.

REFLECTION ACTIVITY:

I encourage you to pause for a moment and breathe and reflect upon your own personal first encounter with grief or loss of a loved one or pet. What age were you? What did you feel? How did you process the shock?

CHAPTER TWO

REALITY

'Someday, someone will walk into your life and make you realise why it never worked out with anyone else.' – Shon Mehta

I first memory of Mick was when I was around 10 or 11 years old. Our families have known each other all our lives. Mick was about 18 at the time. Our family owned a sheep property off the coast of Port Lincoln and we would visit during the September school holidays, shearing time.

At this particular shearing time, my dad had arranged a shearing crew from Mantung, near his home town, approximately 800 kilometres away.

Grief

I was always a bit of a tomboy and loved animals, so much so that I was getting in the way, so dad gave me a stick of marking raddle and told me to go outside and pick out six lambs that I could have—I was so excited! I walked through all the lambs, picking out which ones I wanted, and it kept me occupied for quite some time.

Once I had chosen my six lambs, I proceeded to choose my shearer! I can still remember quite vividly sitting on the rails in the shearing shed watching the shearers to pick out the one I wanted to shear my lambs.

There was one shearer I noticed, he didn't kick the sheep or swear at them—he was kind, so I chose him. His name was Michael Evans (Mick) and I felt a connection between us. He was my childhood crush.

Time passed and we had our separate lives. I grew up in the city and I became drawn to successful-looking businessmen in suits. I met and married Muzza's dad at 23, had Muzz at 24 and separated not long after my 30th birthday. I learned over time that 'clothes don't maketh the man'.

Although Mick and I continued to cross paths at social gatherings between our families, it wasn't until my early 40s that we were both single and reconnected at my grandma's 90th birthday. My younger brother jokingly told Mick I'd always had a crush on him.

The rest, as they say is history!

If I think about my entire adult life, I have been looking for that same feeling of connection since that day and have never found it with anyone but Mick.

2018

The moment the policeman left; Mick poured us both a scotch. I've never been much of a scotch drinker, but we managed to drink more than half a bottle.

I felt stone-cold sober. I was numb. I sat silently at the kitchen table while Mick stayed strong and phoned our friends and family to share the devastating news.

The next few days were a blur of sharing news, phone calls, messages, liaising with police officers and processing the shock.

My younger brother came to the farm, and I was sweeping out under the pergola, so numb I couldn't cry. Later that day when I was inside, I called out for my younger brother to come in and I fell into his arms in tears. I had been trying to hold on to my emotions because if I cried, it would make it all real.

I flew to Queensland and spent hours at the Jimboomba Police Station with my younger brother with the police going through the events surrounding Muzz's death. I visited the property where he had taken his own life. Standing in the spot where he was found felt like something out of a bad movie with no resolution. How could this happen to Muzz?

Today

The years seem to be going faster. I know they say, the older you get, the quicker they go but this feels different. I can't believe it is over five years since Muzz has been gone. It really only feels like a week or so ago, possibly because when it happened, a week felt so long and it was all a blur. One minute, I was relaxing at home, then a policeman came to the farm to tell me my son was dead. Before I had time to process it, I was on a plane to Queensland to pick up some of his belongings and make arrangements for his funeral and to say goodbye. It was all so surreal.

Elizabeth Kubler Ross's five stages of grief are denial, anger, bargaining, depression, and then, finally, acceptance. In those first few days and weeks I went back and forth through all five stages in different times and orders. They are not linear stages and it's common for any of us who are living with grief to find ourselves in each of the stages from time to time.

Although I have accepted Muzz is no longer here in physical form he meets me in my dreams all the time. Even when I am awake, I feel like losing him was all a bad dream, and hope I will wake up from it and Muzz will be with us again. Sometimes my dreams seem so real with Muzz and then I wake up and realise what has happened. This is something so many people relate to when they lose a loved one.

One difficult thing I do often is automatically reach for my phone to call Muzz. I go to call him to tell him some news and then I realise all over again that he is gone, and that I can't do that. In my head, I still hear the phone ring and when I answer I hear his voice, 'hello mummy'. I miss him so much and he is in my head every minute of every hour of every day.

Mary Frances O'Connor's book describes how grief changes everything, that the brain is designed for learning and that the relationship between us and the person who passed must describe who we are now, to be able to restore a meaningful life.

The relationship between Muzz and I is just as strong, but it is a different relationship. It has to be. Because I am not who I used to be before I lost him. I still talk to him and feel he is with me and at the same time I am equally missing him in physical form. The meaningful work I do to help others with their mental health makes me feel closer to him.

The one thing that I have learned is that my priorities have changed and therefore certain things don't matter to me anymore. This has certainly changed some of my relationships with both family and friends, some for the better and some have ended. I've realised life is very short and my time is so valuable.

REFLECTION ACTIVITY:

Everyone processes and expresses how they are feeling differently.

What does grief look like and feel like to you?

This would be a really good place to write in your journal or do a basic meditation to reflect on your own experience of what grief is for you and how that feels throughout your body. Don't fight it, just ease yourself into the emotion/feeling. Be kind to yourself. Make time for yourself.

Bridget Johns is an organisation expert and talks about the 1% theory, a principle that has transformed the lives of her clients in her business Be Simply Free and can do the same for you.

Here's the general principle of the 1% theory: every day gifts you with 1,440 minutes, and that means a mere 14.4 minutes represents just 1% of your day.

Instead of ignoring the things that leave us stressed and annoyed, consider the compounding effect of dedicating 1% of each day to sorting them out. I like to use this same principle for self-care. So, how can you use 1% of your day to process and acknowledge your emotions? Here are some ideas:
- Journaling
- Meditation
- Breathwork
- Walking
- Cooking

CHAPTER THREE

TRYING TO MAKE SENSE OF IT ALL

'No one heals himself by wounding another'
- St. Ambrose

During my healing journey and as I tried to make sense of it all, I thought about how I had spoken to Muzz the day before he took his own life.

He had been driving to his house in Jimboomba to meet with his estranged wife to sign their settlement agreement. They'd had a brief relationship and I never warmed to her whilst they were together. He was hoping to get a resolution and he told me he was glad things would be settled once and for all and he could move forward with his life.

But I never heard from him again.

I tried to call Muzz the following morning as he was going to tell me how their settlement signing had gone. His phone kept going straight to message bank which was most unusual.

I will never forget that, around midday on the Saturday, 6 January 2018, I felt a pull—a cut from my heart. I even wrote about the feeling in my journal and told Mick about it. I thought it was an emotional release.

I now know that I felt him leave.

I often wonder just what unfolded in those 24 hours between speaking to Muzz for the last time and discovering he was gone.

What happened?

Will I ever know the truth?

In an attempt to answer these questions, I arranged to meet with Muzz's estranged wife whilst I was in Queensland organising things while his body was being returned to South Australia.

The meeting did not go well.

My questions remained unanswered and resulted in me yelling 'Murderer!' at her in a coffee shop full of patrons whose jaws were all dropped to the floor.

Not my proudest moment.

But honestly, in my mother's intuition, I have always felt there was more to Muzz's suicide than I will ever truly know.

Why? Why? Why?

I had left a marriage and family of intergenerational domestic violence and felt I had gotten myself and Muzz out to break the cycle. I am grateful that Muzz didn't grow up to be a violent man.

There are people out there who are old, who don't look after themselves, are child abusers and they all get to keep their children.

There are people who take their family for granted and never experience what I have.

When any of us go through grief, we often ask why.

I constantly asked myself what had I done that was so terrible to bring this upon myself.

Was it karma?

Days after we lost Muzz, to function in society, I was prescribed a high dose of antidepressant medication. I couldn't get out of bed and I couldn't sleep the first week after he passed because of the physical pain. My nickname is 'Snooze' and has been most of my life basically because I can sleep through anything and love sleep so this was something that I had never experienced before. I had never felt pain like it and never will again.

Grief and loss can feel like a truly out of body experience.

As I watch Muzz's friends age, get married and have children it often makes me wonder where he would be and what he would be doing. I feel like Muzz was robbed, that I was robbed. Life goes on and it is my burden to bear, not anyone else's.

When navigating grief, sometimes time seems to stand still, sometimes it goes by too quickly and sometimes it all feels so long ago.

Everything I thought I had believed in, I questioned. I was already a self-help book junkie, reading books from Abraham Hicks to Eckhart Tolle but I went even deeper trying to find the answers.

Some days it does make sense, other days I am still in disbelief.

We always have a choice to spiral up or spiral down in our thinking.

My nutritionist said to me one day, 'Suzi, your son is gone, but you are still here, so you need to look after yourself'.

From that moment, I swore that Muzz's death would not be in vain.

CHAPTER FOUR

MUZZA'S HAPPY HOUR

> 'As soon as healing takes place, go out
> and heal somebody else.'
> - Maya Angelou

A few months after Muzz's death, Mick and I went to the local tavern. It was a Sunday and I clearly remember how I still felt emotionally naked when I mixed with people, I was sure people could see right into my broken heart.

There were a couple at the tavern we knew who had lost their son to cancer not long before. The wife sat with me as she could tell I was struggling.

To look into the eyes of another mother who also felt the pain of losing a child was deeply emotional and yet somehow healing. She spoke to me about how people can unintentionally be so cruel. That someone had said to her, 'but you still have three other boys' and another person had commented, 'isn't she over that yet?'

She and I both knew that losing a loved one is an experience that you don't ever get over, you simply try and find a way to walk with it.

She also told me about a time she was in a supermarket and the fear of bumping into someone was so great that she left a full trolley and went home. I was so grateful for this story as it was only a few weeks later I was in the supermarket in Waikerie and the fear of bumping into someone came over me. In that moment, I remembered what she had told me and, funnily enough, I continued with my shopping — just the comfort of knowing that it was okay for me to leave the trolley and go was enough to give me the strength to continue.

It can be small moments like this simple conversation with that friend that can bring us small comfort in our grief. I want to remind you that no matter what you're going through right now, you are not alone.

A few days later, Mick heard of another father who had lost a daughter in a tragedy and was really struggling. Mick said, 'I wish I could just talk to him, I know I could help.'

'I know what we can do!' I replied instantly, 'Let's create a space called "Muzza's happy hour"! A place on a Sunday where people can feel welcome to get together — to talk, not talk, a place just to feel like they belong and find out how to access support.'

The idea was born. So, we started gathering ideas, locations and dates to plan our first get together.

A few months later I was honoured to have my project of Muzza's Happy Hour recognised in the National Rural Women's Coalition e-muster as the only representative for South Australia. It was an amazing experience and a beautiful network of women to support this vision I held.

I am so proud that Muzza's Happy Hour now has its own website as an information vessel for people to access support with mental health, suicide prevention and wellbeing.

Over the past few years, I have also developed my own resilience-building program to support people to uncover their inner resources. The program is called Workbench for the Mind and provides a safe, supportive space where people can uncover their own inner resources or workbench that can be used to improve their wellbeing.

I am so overwhelmed and proud to say that, as I write this book, the Workbench for the Mind program has been accredited by Suicide Prevention Australia.

The WORKBENCH Acronym:

W – WELLBEING	Improving and understanding our wellbeing
O – OPTIMISM	Everyone needs something to look forward to
R – RESILIENCE	To learn how to lean into emotions and the capacity to recover
K – KINDNESS	How to be kinder to yourself
B – BALANCE	Getting everything on our workbench in balance
E – EMOTIONAL INTELLIGENCE	The intelligent use of our emotions – how we manage our behaviour.
N – NEUROSCIENCE	Understanding how our brain and bodies are linked.
C – CARE	Caring for yourself and others – self-care is so important.
H – HOPE	We all need something to hope for

Without an open communication dialogue between generations, communities can't grow or learn from each other. We need to build on the conversations, take it to the next level. Workbench for the Mind gives participants the ability to listen, understand, and communicate effectively, as well as manage their own emotions in positive ways through their emotional workbench.

> **REFLECTION ACTIVITY:**
>
> Visit www.kaizenb.com to download my free Workbench for the Mind work sheet to start to build your own workbench for inner resilience.

CHAPTER FIVE

FORGIVING MYSELF AND OTHERS

'You're in pain. But the thing you lost is the same thing that can stop that pain.'
- Afterlife TV series

Around 300 people came to Muzz's funeral in Waikerie. There is a digital temperature gauge in the main street, and it hit 50 that day. I still remember my sister-in-law saying it was the hottest, saddest day of her life. She summed it up perfectly.

I wasn't prepared for how my relationships would change. I understand now how many people don't know how to support someone through grief, but, when I was going through it, I remember thinking, 'Well, I am the one who is going through it. I am the one who has suffered the loss. Why should you feel uncomfortable?'

I was fortunate to receive so much support from those closest to me. My family unit of friends gave me the most heartfelt gift — a necklace with three charms: the letter M, (for Muzz), 'those we love don't go away, they walk beside us every day" and 'our circle of friendship and love'. I treasure it and wear it every day. My younger brother and his family gave me a gold 'M' necklace (Mummy, Muzz and Mick).

I received some beautiful letters, text messages and phone calls, and I still find comfort in them now. yet some friends that I had known for years didn't even contact me.

I found that sad but I now realise people don't have the resources or understanding to know how to support someone going through grief. Please, if you know someone going through grief or a challenging time, all we want is to know you are there. You don't need to have all the answers, just let them know they aren't alone. Sometimes a thoughtful, handwritten letter means more than we will ever know.

Even saying "I don't know what to say" can be enough.

I feel that I have grown so much emotionally in the past five years. I am in awe of how far I have come, so much further than I ever thought would be possible. I feel so much more aware of my self-talk and, while I still have extremely bad days, by recognising my triggers, I can manage my behaviour and emotions and pull myself out of low moods much more easily. Through my studies in Neuro-Linguistic Programming I've realised I can also learn to let go of the stored emotions around my grief but not have to let go of my memories. My memories of Muzz are always within me.

My mindset has become more of a 'growth mindset' as opposed to a 'fixed mindset' and I recognise how both mindsets work and how each have served me. In her book, *Mindset*, psychologist Carol Dweck says that success comes from having the right mindset rather than intelligence, talent or education. People with a fixed mindset believe that they're born with certain intelligence, skills and abilities that cannot change. People that exhibit a growth mindset, a belief that they have the potential to improve and set less challenging

I recognise I have a choice to stay in a fixed mindset or to grow and move forward. I have a choice to be sad, angry, or any other emotion. I can recognise now that, when I choose to stay in a "down" frame of mind, there is a risk of spiralling down into that mood further. Upon reflection, I can see how much better I am at working through my emotions compared to who I was before I lost Muzz. I am also not concerned about what other people think of me as much as I used to be. I choose to set my goals for me and for Mick and our future together, not for what I felt other people expect of me.

THOUGHTS FOR REFLECTION – CHANGING RELATIONSHIPS

Life is difficult for everyone— no one escapes. I believe everyone goes through their shit. Through my studies in positive psychology, I have learnt that life is not about being positive all the time, but to learn to lean into your pain and grief and allow it, giving you time to rest with it. It is also important to know when it's time to come out and, again, there is no right or wrong.

I don't claim to know it all and I don't claim that everything I know and do is the right thing, but it's right for me.

One of my biggest lessons from losing Muzz and the therapy, counselling and studies I have undertaken, is that I no longer have the time for other people's bullshit. I turn 60 in January 2024 and a friend told me, at this stage of your life, if you haven't sorted out your friendships and your relationships with your family and friends, I don't think you are ever going to. I really believe that so, instead of trying to get people who don't like or respect me or align with my values to like me, I now focus on the people who do love and respect me for who I am—the authentic me, not who they want me to be.

I think the take away from this is to be kind to yourself. I think I lived most of my life in anxiety, certainly most of my childhood at least, and in an era where the mentality was 'toughen up—or to get over it – or back in my day …' You know, it's all our perception, isn't it? It's the lens we view everything through.

I find that people tend to sort their relationships out when a traumatic thing happens in their lives.

One day, someone asked me what I believe in and what are my spiritual beliefs.

The answer is, I don't know.

I used to define myself by others' opinions, but now I have the emotional strength to define myself by my own values. It's quite a freeing experience.

I do believe in something.

I do believe in a higher self.

As to what that is, I don't quite know.

I know science says that there isn't an afterlife, I suppose there are different types of scientists, but I don't know enough about science to explain some of the signs that have happened since Muzz's passing. These signs have let me know he is with me, so is that just my mind wishing the signs were Muzz, or are they real?

Mick believes it doesn't matter, that if it helps me to believe, then believe. I like the thought of that.

So, I am still on that part of my journey, and it is a work in progress.

Aside from being healing for me, this book is to share my learnings in a simple format. Grief is a very private thing to go through and I believe a lot of people don't understand that because they want to help. I know it frustrates the hell out of many who want to be there for me, but this is something that can't be fixed. Grief is such a little word yet there is so much behind it, so many layers.

THE DIFFERENT TYPES OF GRIEF

There are many different types of grief. Some of these are:

- Grief for a life lost
- Grief for a relationship
- Grief for what could have been
- Grief of money lost
- Grief of time lost

Grief can also be from an experience. Whether it's separation or divorce, a lost connection with a sibling, an estranged child, a broken friendship or a miscommunication.

When parents separate or divorce, I don't think parents give enough consideration to the ripple effect the divorce has.

I'm not saying they shouldn't divorce — there are often very valid reasons why the relationship must end, like my relationship with Muzz's dad.

I don't believe you can have divorced parents and still have a family unit. You will have another kind of family unit but it's not the same family unit because the mothers and fathers from that divorce will go on and find other partners, and potentially have other children. The family dynamic changes and it becomes more complicated. There is grief to consider in all these changes especially for children trying to get use to their new way of life.

I left my abusive marriage to Muzz's father when Muzz was aged seven, a few months after my 30th birthday. Muzz was a beautiful soul who witnessed and experienced physical abuse in his early childhood. The things he witnessed and experienced as a child could not be undone even with my divorce. It was hard, but it was a decision I am so proud I had the strength to make. I know I gave Muzz the best possible chance at a different future because I chose us. I received no divorce settlement and minimal child support until the last few years before Muzz turned 18. I have had to learn to forgive myself for the experiences I couldn't prevent Muzz from having in his early childhood.

At some stage we all need to forgive ourselves and those who have hurt us knowing that we are all only doing the best we can with what we know at the time.

Punishing ourselves and others only prolongs the pain.

> **REFLECTION ACTIVITY:**
>
> Do something kind for yourself today as an act of self-care and forgiveness for your past self and the choices and decisions you made at the time.
>
> Research says that helping others can be good for our own mental health. It can reduce stress and improve our own emotional well-being so why not pay it forward - try a random act of kindness for someone else today.

CHAPTER SIX

MOVING FORWARD

'I don't know because everyone's situation is different... You can't try to control it. It's going to happen or it's happening. You let go and you go through it. If you constantly fight it, and you constantly resist it, you are going to spend your whole life fighting. And you are going to be at the end of your life thinking, 'I don't remember the times of calm and peace,' because you have created a fight. Everyone is going to be hit with something. And just when you think it's over, you are going to get hit again. You just hope that you have people in your life who are going to show you the light at the end of the tunnel if you can't see it.'
- Sandra Bullock

Just as Mick and I were starting to see our way through the fog of grief, we were blindsided again.

We had finished shearing on the farm on the Friday and on the Saturday, we had been out in the afternoon and when we came home, Mick said he was going to bed early. Something wasn't right because he was so tired, he couldn't even undo the lid off the tube of toothpaste. He had no strength.

The next morning, Mick woke me at 5.00am, saying something was wrong and that he needed to go to the hospital (said no farmer ever!). We were about 15kms of the way through the 70km journey to hospital, and he said, 'I think you need to call an ambulance'.

That's when I got scared. Later he told me he thought he was having a stroke.

He was diagnosed with Guillain Barre Syndrome which is when your immune system attacks your peripheral nerves. He was paralysed from the neck down.

He spent six months in hospital and had to learn to walk again.

I was told at first that he could die, and I remember crying in the hospital corridor at 3:00am, looking up and screaming, 'you can't take Mick too'. I really questioned what was going on—was I really that bad a person that all the people I loved were being taken from me?

The doctors told me he would be in a wheelchair or a home for life. I didn't tell Mick—I didn't know how—and thank God I didn't as we both truly believe a big part of his recovery was that he didn't know that he most likely wouldn't walk again. He dug deep and put everything into his recovery to meet his goals of living on the farm and running the farm again.

Mick was in a wheelchair when he came home which took its toll on both of us—such a strong, independent man having to depend on me for everything in the beginning. He grieved for the time lost in the hospital, for the time that was taken from him to do what he wanted to on the farm.

That must have been so painful for him — I know it was for me to observe.

I felt that it was best for Mick to write about his own experience with grief:

Mick's story

It's strange the thoughts that go through your mind when you receive the news of a loved one losing their life.

I felt sorry for the poor cop who had to tell us what happened to Muzz that night in 2018.

As soon as I heard the news about Muzz I immediately thought, 'What is Suzi going to do?' He took his own life — I felt angry at the world.

The realisation came that this has happened, and it's happened to us.

You always hear about these things, and it is always someone else. Not us.

The next three weeks from the night we received the news were a blur.

Life goes on, we still had to do our day-to-day tasks as we had a business to run. We also had to bring Muzz back from Queensland and organise the funeral.

We didn't have a lot of time to think about anything other than putting one foot in front of the other.

It was after the funeral that the reality really hit home. We still had to continue and function.

As suicide is still a taboo subject, most people found it really hard to talk to Suzi. I found it a little hard for a while but, being in the middle of it, you realise it is a mental health issue and I felt so much for the pain he must have been going through.

Suzi's strength was great as she said I suggested (more than suggested) that she get out of bed in the morning and wash her face, have breakfast then she could go back to bed if she wanted but she had to get up and do those things first.

For a start, I used to come home to check and very rarely was she still in bed. The courage she showed just getting up every day was amazing.

Grief

I threw myself into work and our community hall as that was the only escape I had for a while.

She had amazing friends, but they can only do so much. It was the times that we were alone that could have quite easily torn us apart.

We were going through some shit years on the land, but it seemed a bit easier for me to get through, knowing what Muzz must have been experiencing to do what he did.

Suzi got to the stage where she started setting her goals for the future and she wanted to include Muzz in that too.

She worked really hard to set up Muzza's Happy Hour, studied hard and set up her own mental health training business.

Around 18 months after we lost Muzz, things were really looking up. Suzi was getting back to her normal self. I know she will never be the same again but, to her credit, she is coping. It must be so hard for a mother to lose her only son. Every day still has its challenges. I know it's bad enough for me so I can only imagine what she must be going through.

We were going for a walk early one morning, I was talking about how things were looking up and I was feeling quite good.

Then a week later, everything changed when I ended up in hospital.

I was paralysed from the neck down within a matter of days and diagnosed with an uncommon disease, Guillain Barre Syndrome, that I was (un)lucky enough to pick up in its worst form.

During my rehabilitation and lengthy recovery, it was hard at times to keep motivated. I knew that I was the only one that could dig deep enough to get myself out of this hole.

I never felt so scared when trying to walk. At times it almost became overwhelming and sometimes I couldn't do what I had done the day before.

The first time I was able to roll over in bed by myself was an amazing feeling. Then I got to the stage that I could use the slide board from the bed into the wheelchair and shower myself, then pester them to let me get into the gym or somewhere else.

All this time, Suzi's support was the one thing that helped to kept me going.

After a lot of practice, I got to the stage where I could get from the wheelchair into the car, and Suzi took me out to lunch. We had fish and chips down by the river, but I realised I wasn't ready to go home — I had to go back to hospital.

I could see so much that I needed to be doing and couldn't physically do it, once again I put my head down and kept work, work, working. Eventually, some of my little wins became bigger and I started to become more independent, which must have been a great relief for Suzi.

It has been four years now that I've been back doing virtually everything on the farm, not quite as confidently as I used to. I still have my dark moments, but I try not to let them override so many good moments.

I have achieved most of my goals. My ankles don't work properly, and I can't wriggle my toes which is more annoying than impeding me. I think I am still regaining strength so I will keep pushing on,

I've still got to dig deep and remind myself, don't let the bastards win!

I don't know where I found the belief and determination to keep getting up after every set back, but it came, and I am so glad that it did.

As strange as it sounds, I feel that all of this has actually brought us closer together.

I am so proud of Suzi and I because, for either of us, it would have been so easy to go down the track of giving up and hitting the bottle or finding some other escape you could find.

- Mick (Suzi's husband and Muzz's step father)

CHAPTER SEVEN

YOU CAN'T POUR FROM AN EMPTY CUP

'I realise that everyone's struggling, and I feel like I should help the people who helped me. That's what life is all about.'
(Quote from *Afterlife*)

My mum always said Muzz was like a big Labrador.

He would plod along or bound in and turn around and his tail would knock everything over. Muzz always used to say, 'Mum, you're such a Wally', so I knew in my heart I wanted to get a dog someday and name him Wally. Mick was concerned about me emotionally if something were to happen to the dog I might not ever recover. But in my heart, I knew I wanted to feel that love again and so I decided to get a dog for me and my own healing.

A year after Muzz passed, I travelled to Adelaide to choose my puppy (originally named Jumbo La La). There was a little black female pup in the litter and so I cuddled her too, but Jumbo didn't like it! He went crazy, whining and jumping up like he was telling me, 'No, I am your puppy, not her!' I picked him up again and then they were all put to bed. When I left, I turned around said, 'see ya, Wally!' and Jumbo jumped up, so that was it!

Wally is 50kg of unconditional love. He is beautiful. He has healed parts of me and I feel like he is Muzz in a furry form. Muzz gave the best "Bear hugs" and Wally is just like a big bear!

THOUGHTS FOR REFLECTION – PUTTING YOURSELF FIRST VS BEING SELFISH

I always thought that putting myself first was being selfish. I now know that there is a difference between the two. If we put ourselves and our own self-care first, we will be in a better position to be more helpful to those around us.

To me, putting myself first is about myself taking care of me and my immediate environment and surroundings where the intent is not from a place of scheming or inconsideration or selfish motives. In fact, it is about my mental peace, my self-respect, my self-love, my morals and values and it is a responsibility to myself so by putting myself first I am then being kind to those around me. In my life, this is where my passion and values for my business have come in, wanting people to take care of themselves so that they can be the best version of themselves. Then it has to have a flow on or ripple effect—it just has to. I'm sure you know the sayings, 'put your own oxygen mask on first' and 'you can't pour from an empty cup'.

It's not my job to be a counsellor to others, but it is my job to be a friend. One thing I have learned from the mental health study is that it's not about fixing people — that isn't my job. My job is to guide people to get the support and help they need.

I think sometimes people see me doing well and go, 'oh, she can help fix me' but they don't see the dark days, the down days. It's not my job to fix people, my role as I see it is to give people the tools and guidance to help themselves. That is what I believe is missing in our society now. I believe this is the ultimate act of self-care, to not spend your energy fixing others but rather, show them the way to do it for themselves.

Over the last six years, my emotions have been somewhat of a roller coaster and moving around the meaning of life as my daily situation changes. I go from feeling positive and really on track of where I am heading to having a rough day, and wondering what I am doing. I now find it easier to get through the rough days by acknowledging my emotions and leaning into them. Then, by understanding my triggers, I find that I can manage my reactions to my emotions and channel my anxiety into a more positive action by focusing on my business and spending time putting together my workshops and business development. It makes me feel good that I am reaching and helping so many people.

It's not about being happy all the time—life doesn't work that way—however, with finding our strengths and living to our own values, we have the tools to manage our emotions and cope with life's challenges in a more productive way.

REFLECTION ACTIVITY:

Where could you put yourself and your healing first? What is something you desire and have perhaps not allowed yourself?

CHAPTER EIGHT

LIVING IN THE NOW

> 'Faith is so specific for who you are. There is no right or wrong way to have gratitude, or to pray, or to ask for help, or to talk to someone who might not be there; if it brings you calm and it brings you strength, it's the right thing to do. It doesn't have to be in the house of God, it could be sitting on your couch, or outside under a tree.'
> - Sandra Bullock

When I was a little girl, I had comfort in sleeping with my teddy bears. I can remember one night there was a storm, so I put *all* of them (around 20!) in my bed and then there was no room for me so I had to sleep on the floor!

Grief

After Muzz passed, I found myself sleeping with my teddy bears again. They surrounded my body and it was a great comfort — how the mind can take us back to a time when we felt safe.

Something I started to do to calm myself down is picture a magnet inside of me. What I think and focus on is what the magnet attracts. This helps me to stop myself from spiralling down.

Now, night-time gives me peace. After Mick has gone to bed, I watch one or two episodes of Afterlife and it's like no one can reach me. It's too late for the phone to ring — peace in the silence.

When you change, especially after a period of heavy grief, some people aren't accepting of the change, yet others allow you to change and are there no matter what. I understand that everyone has their struggles and that no one escapes but the kindness that has been bestowed on me has been humbling. It makes me want to be a better, calmer, kinder person and that is what I try and do each day — not to measure or judge myself against others but against myself, not to live up to other people's values but to mine. Just because they are different doesn't mean anyone is right or wrong—they are just different, and I have learned to live by mine to be a better version of myself than I was yesterday.

Frances O'Connor describes the difference between grief and grieving.

She says that grief really is a feeling where you have the sort of intensity that just overwhelms you and is more of a momentary experience. Grieving, on the other hand, is the way that grief changes over time without ever actually going away. She goes on to say that, the first 100 times, you get knocked off your feet by that feeling of grief, that wave of grief. The 101st time you feel it, it may be just as awful, but it may also be familiar, so now you may have some ways to comfort yourself, or you may know how to reach out to someone in that moment.

Even though the feeling hasn't really changed, the relationship to the feeling changes over time. If we expect that we are not going to feel grief in the future and that somehow, it's going to be over, then we will be disappointed if, years later, we come across something or a situation and suddenly we get all emotional and have that overwhelming feeling of grief. That doesn't mean that, at that moment, we were aware of the loss of something really important.

The grieving heart pines for the loved one to be back or for things to be back the way they were before. We now know from both diagnostic clinical sciences, but also brain imaging work that grief and depression are not the same thing.

Of course, I feel shattered that Muzz isn't here anymore, and experience bouts of depression. I might feel guilty about things I've done and worry about the way I communicate with people.

Grieving really focuses on needing that loved one to be back. I feel as though I can go on without Muzz in my life so it's a different experience.

Our brain embeds the bond of when we fall in love, so it chooses a 'we', not a you and I, and therefore when our spouse or child or other loved one dies or is gone it feels like we have lost a part of who we are — it feels so real.

Mary Frances O'Connor explains that we can link this similarity to the phantom limb syndrome, so if someone has had an arm or part of a leg amputated, they will sometimes experience some feeling of itching or pain in the absent limb. We understand that this is because the brain has not yet rewired itself to the acceptance of the limb being gone. The same with the tragic loss of a loved one.

She also goes on to explain the analogy of, if we break our arm or leg, we don't do anything to specifically mend those pieces back together—a natural healing process takes care of that. We might support the limb while it mends with a plaster cast or use crutches or a sling. This is the same in that grief is a natural response to loss. It is what our brain, our mind, and our body do in reaction to the loss.

George Bonino's work says the majority of us will find a way to restore this meaningful life and find a way to live our everyday lives, like loving our grandkids, getting dinner on the table and getting out to the grocery store. So, we try and focus on building new skills in ourselves when we have been derailed in our natural grieving process and we use these new skills to get back to that healing trajectory. This is not designed to get us to stop grieving but more to take care of ways that we have become derailed, like thoughts we are having, behaviours we are having in response to our emotions that are not helping us to manage our emotions more effectively and move forward. No matter how awful grief feels, it is still completely different to focusing on what happened at the moment of death or when we finally come to the realisation that this person just isn't coming back.

Grief can be so painful that some people experiencing it avoid situations, reminders or people they associate with their loved one. The problem with avoidance is it tends to manifest as more avoidance so sometimes we start to avoid more and more things that remind us of this painful grief.

So, in trying to make sense of what life might be like now without our loved one, we have to learn what makes sense for us now, and what is meaningful to us. For the brain to learn, we need to have new experiences. So, for me and my family, we started having every second Christmas at a beach house, generating new memories/experiences.

Support and encouragement are most beneficial to embark on new behaviours so that our brain learns that life is full of many possibilities.

It is important for you to have a positive support system working with you and that they understand to the best of their ability what you are going through. Then, they can try and provide support to you and not back off from your overwhelming grieving emotions.

Research suggests that yearning declines and that acceptance increases, but this doesn't always happen in a set kind of way, these are just the moments where people are aware of their grief. Everyone's experience is completely different, there is no right or wrong.

Then we have ambiguous loss, which it can be so challenging. Ambiguous loss is the sense of loss and sadness that is not because of a death, it is more of a loss of an emotional connection when the person is still physically with us. Or, it can be when there is a physical loss and the person is emotionally still with us, which can mean that there is no closure like we have when someone dies. An example of this is knowing someone with dementia—the person is still physically with us but emotionally gone, so we experience an array of mixed emotions.

So, when we have a memory and an everlasting relationship with someone, the automatic solution would be to simply just go find them if they are not in our presence. When we realise, we can't do that, it can cause upset and confusion and be a reason why it is such a long process to grieve.

THOUGHTS FOR REFLECTION – ACCEPTANCE VERSUS CHANGE

It is what it is—accepting that you can't change the situation, however, you are changed forever. My dear friends Tony and Pat lost their son, Ben, to tragic circumstances when he was around two years old. When Muzz passed, Tony said to me, 'You will be okay. You will never be the same again, but you will be okay'.

A lot of the books I have read and podcasts listened to say to accept or change the situation you are in, but this is sometimes easier said than done. I do feel connection with this advice, so if we accept the situation, we can be more open to change or, in my case, it relieved a lot of stress for me. Acceptance brings with it the release of not stressing about the future and what will happen and the stress of not being able to change the past.

For me, the idea of acceptance meant not fighting. Somewhere, subconsciously, I was fighting that Muzz was still out there somewhere, that it had all been a mistake and a bad dream and acceptance meant it was real and that I had to deal with it. It meant that I had to finally come to terms with it and make decisions of what my life was to become.

It also frightened me because I didn't want to be happy, because how could I be happy when my son was dead? I felt guilty when I was happy, so I would not allow myself to be. That didn't necessarily mean that I was depressed or down, but I just couldn't give myself permission to accept the loss of Muzz. In my mind, changing my life, not for better or worse, just change, meant I would forget him. I now know that that can never be as he is in my mind 24/7 and, no matter what I do, that will never change. However, what has had to change is for me to create a life for myself without Muzz physically being here. My relationship with him is still strong, he is just with me emotionally and not physically — ah, the layers of grief.

Your experience with grief and the people you miss or have lost gives you the opportunity to redefine your connection and relationship with these people. To become a stronger version of you and yet at the same time to feel more vulnerable and real in this world.

In Japanese culture, the term *Kintsugi* means to make something new from a broken pot, which is transformed to possess a different sort of beauty. The imperfection, the golden cracks, are what make the new object unique. I believe we are transformed through our experiences and grief and therefore hold a different sort of beauty in this world.

CONCLUSION

I CHOOSE ME

'Everything can be taken from a man but one thing: the last of the human freedom— to choose one's attitude in any given set of circumstances, to choose one's own way.' - Victor E. Frankl

The above quote from Victor E. Frankl really stayed with me after reading his book *Man's Search for Meaning*. I found that he watched the signs and triggers of those around him in the concentration camp and seemed to know when someone was about to die. Somehow, he was determined to not let the Nazis get to him, and kept faith that they could not take from him his right to choose. He couldn't control the situation he was in however, he could control his mindset, his attitude. It gave him purpose and meaning to keep going. It was motivating to me how he did this. He was in such horrific conditions and experiences, yet he didn't lose his faith in himself.

When trying to find one's meaning in life, there isn't any one way. It is about having a sense of purpose, to live in line with your values. I have found that, during my studies, I have been focusing more on living up to my values, not on other people's. Meaning doesn't just appear; it is something we create through doing exactly that — living to our own values.

Grief changes you. There is not a second of any day that I do not have Muzz in my thoughts — it is how it is now — but I choose to live and make his life worthwhile. I choose to honour Muzz and to help others and, through grieving, I want to be more authentic and be a better person, but not at my own expense. The reality is that we are all different with different values and we live in a western world where we have the right to our own opinions. In my opinion, we should live more to our own values, not to others values, as that is not being true to ourselves.

I look at all the self-help books I have and swear I won't buy another one and I often wonder, why do we trust a stranger and what they have written rather than our own intuition? I suppose we first need the education to know about our own intuition. I feel I have always had that intuition and whenever I have not listened to it is when things go wrong for me.

When you peel away the layers and have the power to be your authentic self, then your world opens up. When you do, some of your relationships change or end and that is a grieving experience in itself as you find yourself having to choose between what was and what is and what can be. So, I choose me. I am slowly letting more back into my emotional protective circle but for now I am getting to know me and it feels good.

My business Kaizen Business Support makes me feel closer to Muzz somehow. He would have been so good at this work, and I had to be careful that I wasn't becoming addicted to grief or to my work in the sense that it was a way to escape. I suppose in one sense it is, however, not to the detriment of me or Mick. I had to check in with myself a lot to make sure I was doing it for the right reasons and that my intentions were clear.

Kaizen translates to a Japanese business philosophy of continuous improvement and this is what my life now reflects.

Most days it is everything for me to put one foot in front of the other but, through understanding my emotions and how my brain works and is linked to my body, I manage my behaviour to my emotions more effectively. That, along with medication, a good psychologist and, most importantly, with my farmer Mick, I put one foot in front of the other.

My wish is that this book guides you with support for your grief and enables you to put one foot in front of the other and move forward. Please head to my website at www.kaizenb.com to download my free Workbench for the Mind work sheet to support you further.

Choose *you*! I chose me because the alternative is a dark hole that I don't think I would ever get out of and then all the people and situations that I feel have wronged me win, so fuck them — I choose *me*!

I hope you decide to *choose you*!

> Love and light
> Suzi Evans

'Life can be heavy. Especially, if you try to carry all at once. Part of growing up and moving into new chapters of your life, it's about catch and release. You can't carry all things, all grudges, decide what's yours to hold, let the rest go.'

Taylor Swift

Grief

A love that knows no bounds..
A care that does not even understand complacency..
Strength that could conquer the biggest army.. but is implemented with the softest of hands..
Her happiness comes from me being happy..
Her word, 28 years on, still rules..
Her success is entwined with mine..
because i am her son.. and she, my mother..
Through thick and thin.
A love unconditional, still lives on...
Love ya snooze.
Happy mothers day, your son, Muzz.

Suzanne Evans

To my amazing mummy!
Happy Birthday, another year down and another year I am so proud to be your son, and as a son to be so proud of you.

I am the luckiest kid around to have a mum who is so understanding, loving and caring. We have been through so much. and when I look back now, I realise how lucky I was to have a mother who went through so much and did so much for me. and please know I will never forget that. but through the past and into the future please be proud of yourself and what you have done, because through it all you are going strong... so... and Jus thanks to your Suzi Q, Michael Angelo, Nikki, Giovanni, turn one page and thats my mummy!

I love you with all my heart mum. XOXO

today is
all about ewe!

happy BiRtHDay

Grief

WALLY

Suzanne Evans

Grief

4 NEWS
The Loxton News, Wednesday, August 22, 2018

'Suicide didn't kill my son'

It has been almost nine months since Mantung woman Suzi Evans received the news that no parent wants and every mother dreads. It was a warm summer's evening when the police drove down the dusty Mallee driveway to let Suzi know her son, her 'Muzza', and her world as she knew it, was gone. Today Suzi has shared her story with *Loxton News* editor Stephanie Thompson in a bid to break the stigma surrounding depression in the hope it will help others.

It was Monday, January 8 this year when Suzi and her husband, Mick, saw the police car driving towards their farm home.

"I suppose somewhere deep inside I knew that something was wrong, but it was all so surreal," she said.

"You hear of people saying that everything is in slow motion and that it is an out-of-body experience."

"Well they're not wrong; it was like a scene out of a movie."

Words and phrases such as "took his own life" and "committed suicide" were used in the conversations that followed in coming days as Suzi prepared to bring her son, Murray Chesser, home from Queensland.

He was just 29 years young.

"He didn't die from suicide – he died from depression," Suzi said.

"You haven't got healthy people walking down the street deciding to take their life.

"You have depressed people, who decide suicide will end the pain because of their depression."

Each day, more than eight Australians die by suicide.

"What are we doing as a society about it?" Suzi said.

"We aren't talking about it, we are shoving it under the carpet."

The level of taboo surrounding depression and suicide in our society was highlighted when Suzi was often asked if the funeral service would be private.

"It was just like, 'What do you mean?'," she said.

"Then they would say, 'Well, because it was a suicide'."

"Why would I make it a private funeral?"

> **He didn't die from suicide – he died from depression. You haven't got healthy people walking down the street deciding to take their life.**

Instead, Murray's family requested those attending wear bright colours in honour of his life.

"Firstly, his life deserved to be celebrated, but secondly, people need to be aware that this is happening," Suzi said.

"We had a few people we knew who were not going to let their sons of similar age – who are struggling with depression – attend the funeral.

"But, we said, 'No, you have to, you have to see this is what happens. This is the result'."

Suzi said she was concerned society's current methods of dealing with depression and suicide were not working.

"I just can't believe that we don't discuss it," she said.

"You would then assume the suicide rate would be going down, but it isn't, so that's not working."

Each year, about 3000 Australians die by suicide, with deaths among males occurring at a rate three times greater than that of females.

For every death by suicide, it is estimated that as many as 30 people attempt to end their lives.

Suzi said society is quick to judge when suicide is determined as the cause of death.

"I think, when he died, a lot of people went, 'Oh well, it's drugs' because he had been involved."

"But, it wasn't."

Murray had suffered from depression for years and Suzi said alcohol – and drugs later on – became his coping vices.

"I didn't know everything about my son, but I did know him pretty well and Maze didn't do drugs because he was a druggy," she said.

"He had depression and was trying to get rid of the pain."

The excessive drinking numbed it for a while and then that wasn't enough, so he went to the drugs.

"He was a strong person and got himself out of that and did so for three years."

Despite being free from drugs years prior to his death, Suzi said she still wondered if drugs had played a part in his death.

"But, it wasn't," she said.

"There were no drugs or alcohol in his system or any sign of it.

"He turned his life around from drugs and was in Queensland as that's where his dad was."

Suzi said at times, it might have been easier to deal with his passing if he was under the influence at his time of death.

"We almost hoped he had," she said.

"No one wants to think that their child would choose to not come and ask for help and would rather end their life.

"He tried through the drugs to kill himself and it didn't work, then he lived sober and chose that he didn't want to be here.

"At the end of the day, I don't respect his choice, but I accept his choice, I have to."

Suzi often finds herself smiling when asked to describe her son.

"He was larger than life," she said.

"My mum summed him up beautifully when she said he was like a big labrador puppy.

"He was a real character."

Murray spent time living in the Riverland, playing football and missed netball for Waikerie and was a qualified carpenter.

"He loved what he did," Suzi said.

Suzi said the past months had felt like a "bad dream".

"I thought I was handling it well, but probably only three or four weeks ago, I felt I was only coming out of the shock then," she said.

"It's like you never knew you were sick until you feel better again.

"For me, I suppose it was whenever the phone used to ring, I would think, 'Oh, that's him', but now I know that will never be."

Suzi said she hoped talk about depression continues and encouraged those suffering to seek help.

"We have to do something – awareness, education, change our key words, I don't know," she said.

"I don't know the answers, but it just astounds me the amount of people in this country who take their life.

"If 3000 people a year were drowning in the sea, beaches would be shut until they found out the cause."

If you or a loved one are having thoughts of suicide, contact Lifeline on 13 11 14 or Beyondblue on 1300 224 636.

Want freight tomorrow?

Reliable, trustworthy, overnight freight from Adelaide to the Riverland with Sprint Freight

Suzi to honour son and support grieving parents

by Stephanie Thompson

A local woman will implement a gathering for parents who have lost a child, following a leadership program in Canberra recently.

Manning's Suzi Evans was one of 12 women selected for the National Rural Women's Coalition's Canberra Muster Leadership program earlier this month.

Following the program, participants are required to develop a project which has a positive impact on rural, regional and remote women.

For Mrs Evans, her project is 'Muzza's happy hour' in honour of her son, who struggled with depression and died by suicide last year.

"One thing I noticed is that while there is suicide prevention and R U OK? days – and they are fantastic and so important in our communities – I found the people I was directly working with hadn't lost a child," she said.

Mrs Evans said following the loss of her son, she found comfort in other parents who have also lost children.

"It doesn't take your pain away, but it makes you feel understood," she said.

"To look into the eyes of another mother who has lost a child is really daunting, but it is also quite empowering and healing at the same time."

Mrs Evans said 'Muzza's happy hour' will start at the Wunkar Tavern in the near future.

"It's just for one hour and you can bring yourself or a friend that you are worried about who has lost a child, not necessarily to suicide," she said.

"It could be illness, from an accident or an act of violence.

"Just for one hour to feel understood, and as though they belong."

Mrs Evans said she hopes to see 'Muzza's happy hour' rolled out across the country for suicide and grief awareness.

As part of the Rural, Regional and Remote Women's Canberra Muster, Mrs Evans spent a day at Parliament House, meeting with Minister for Agriculture Bridget McKenzie, Member for Barker Tony Pasin and other politicians.

The four-day leadership and capacity-building program also encompassed a range of speakers, who shared their personal leadership experience, including how to frame an advocacy issue, bring an issue to the attention of policy makers, working politically, shaping public opinion, and strategies to have voices heard.

Manning's Suzi Evans recently took part in the Rural, Regional and Remote Women's Canberra Muster, hosted by the National Rural Women's Coalition. As part of the four-day leadership and capacity-building program, Mrs Evans caught up with Member for Barker Tony Pasin. PHOTO: supplied

References

After Life (TV series) https://screenrant.com/quotes-ricky-gervais-after-life/#:~:text="I%20Feel%20Like%20I%20Should,The%20People%20Who%20Helped%20Me."&text=At%20one%20point%2C%20he%20says,what%20life%20is%20all%20about.

Beautiful Boy (book) by David Sheff https://www.oprah.com/oprahshow/book-excerpt-from-beautiful-boy-by-david-sheff/16#:~:text=No%20matter%20what%20we%20do,finally%20chose%20life%20for%20myself.

Bridget Johns (1% theory)https://www.mamamia.com.au/organisation-expert/

Kayne West (song) Hey Mamma https://www.google.com/search?client=safari&rls=en&q=kayne+west+hey+mamma&ie=UTF-8&oe=UTF-8#wptab=si:ALGXSlaqmEzXP-BTuaSuCvblodZyXkKSMAGRjFsw0n3X-lbdEvbZMF4ZCYtDeZbJCso-

WygE_S_05F3b84S0mTkmUCZfV-HjRrNZ
9Pt74hGHlqJOdrlJ4ECQTKuj5RRNrm7TAv
4e_RpI6rCZ-o6D4opIpiodrenU8lZvlJ6_ECta_
oQhCEIm5cf0%3D

Kintsugi (meaning) https://theconversation.com/how-the-philosophy-behind-the-japanese-art-form-of-kintsugi-can-help-us-navigate-failure-193487#:~:text=Kintsugi%20makes%20something%20new%20from,make%20the%20new%20object%20unique.

Lisa Marie Presley (essay) https://people.com/music/lisa-marie-presley-was-destroyed-by-son-benjamins-death-grief-essay/

Man's Search for Meaning (book) by Viktore E. Frankl https://www.goodreads.com/quotes/51356-everything-can-be-taken-from-a-man-but-one-thing

Sandra Bullock (quote) https://www.risenmagazine.com/sandra-bullock-perseverance-adversity/#:~:text="Faith%20is%20so%20specific%20for,the%20right%20thing%20to%20do.

Taylor Swift (quote): https://indianexpress.com/article/lifestyle/life-positive/my-mistakes-led-to-the-best-taylor-swift-8229299/#:~:text=%E2%80%9CLife%20can%20 be%20heavy%2C%20especially,and%20what%20things%20to%20release.

The Grieving Brain(book) by Mary Frances O'Connor https://ma ryfrancesoconnor.org/book

You Got It (song)- Roy Orbison (song)https://www.google.com/search?client=safari&rls=en&q=roy+orbison+you+got+it&ie=UTF-8&oe=UTF-8#wptab=si:ALGXSlaqmEzXP-BTuaSuCvblodZyXkKSMAGRjFsw0n3X-lbdEvbZMF4ZCYtDeZbJCsoWygH8-P6z-HD5SwyZyOYU4EFexFXp_xZkqnoQtWMdj5_IMz0d4p9vQZu9uHkqPyD13az1H74sSxL_CJuaF1sQKYM1wqsdkpzUYB_sySpXI1e8MNhoRNE%3D

Support and resources

1. https://www.kaizenb.com

    a. Workbench for the mind https://www.kaizenb.com/workbench-for-the-mind
    b. Mental health first aid training courses (standard, youth, teen) https://www.kaizenb.com/mhfa-training
    c. One on one coaching with Suzi https://www.kaizenb.com/one-on-one-coaching

2. Muzz's Happy Hour https://www.muzzashappyhour.com

3. Beyond Blue https://www.beyondblue.org.au

4. Lifeline https://www.lifeline.org.au

5. Juliet Lever Relaunch My Life (Evolve and Relaunch Education) https://julietlever.com

About the author

SUZI EVANS lives with her husband Mick on their sheep property in South Australia's Murray Mallee. Being dry mallee farmers, they thought they knew resilience well, but their lives took two almighty tragic blows within 18 months, leaving both struggling to find meaning and purpose. After much soul searching, Suzi trained as an instructor and coach in the mental health arena and established her own business. Her work is now accredited by Suicide Prevention Australia.

In this raw and powerful retelling of her journey through gut-wrenching grief, Suzi shares her story of the trauma of losing her son, Muzz, to suicide. Through her heartbreaking experience, Suzi has gained the strength and resilience to help others make sense of theirs, offering a compassionate and genuine guide to navigating grief, reassuring readers that they are not alone. She provides invaluable tools, from positive psychology to mental health first aid, and reminds readers to choose themselves, because every step towards healing begins with a choice.

If you are grieving the loss of a loved one or pet, the loss of a relationship, the loss of time due to illness or estrangement, or the loss of the life you thought you were going to live, this book is for you.

Reach out to here at www.kaizenb.com
for details about upcoming
workshops and training.

KAIZEN
business support

Thank You

Thank You For Reading My Book!

I really appreciate all of your feedback, and I love hearing what you have to say.

I need your input to make the next version of this book and my future books even better.

Please leave me a helpful review on Amazon letting me know what you thought of the book.

Thank you so much!
Suzi Evans

www.ingramcontent.com/pod-product-compliance
Lightning Source LLC
Chambersburg PA
CBHW072016290426
44109CB00018B/2253